CONTAINER TOPIARY

CONTAINER TOPIARY

SUSAN BERRY

Photographs by Steven Wooster

LAUREL
GLEN

San Diego, California

Laurel Glen Publishing
An imprint of the Advantage Publishers Group
5880 Oberlin Drive, San Diego, CA 92121-4794
www.laurelglenbooks.com

ISBN 1-57145-924-3

Library of Congress Cataloging-in-Publication Data
Berry, Susan, 1944-
    Container topiary / Susan Berry ; photographs Steven Wooster.
    p. cm.
    ISBN 1-57145-924-3
    1. Topiary work. 2. Container gardening. I. Title.

SB463 .B47 2003
715'.1--dc21

                                                          2002030098

Printed in Malaysia
1 2 3 4 5 06 05 04 03

Conceived and produced by Berry & Co.
47 Crewys Road, London NW2 2AU
Designer: Debbie Mole
Illustrations: Kate Simunek

Senior Editor: Clare Johnson
Editorial Direction: Rosemary Wilkinson
Production: Hazel Kirkman

CONTENTS

INTRODUCTION

above: *The neatly rounded form of a small topiary box ball (Buxus sp.) provides the anchoring structure for a group of small plants on a tabletop, under the rustic profusion of a clematis bower.*

opposite: *Formality is the rule for this neatly composed display of two bay standards (Laurus nobilis), underplanted with helxine (Solierolia solierolii) and connected by a window box planted up with a lavender (Lavandula dentata) standard and small box balls.*

THE ANCIENT ART OF TOPIARY—the geometric shaping of trees and shrubs—is a core design feature in classical gardens. Mention of topiary was made in ancient Rome by Pliny the Elder (A.D. 23–79), who traced its invention to a friend of Julius Caesar's, and many Roman estates featured clipped and trained plants of some description. The skill disappeared until medieval times when fruit trees were trained against the walls of enclosed gardens. But it was not until the Renaissance that topiary became more widespread. The great Italian gardens produced parades of peacocks, bears, and ships; holes were cut in hedges to frame breathtaking views; and trees were trained so that their branches intertwined (which was known as "pleaching").

In an attempt to demonstrate man's superiority over nature (the principle behind the classical French gardens of the seventeenth century), gardeners trained shrubs and trees into a wide range of symmetrical shapes, which were then used to create classical vistas. Elegant obelisks of clipped dark yew marked the entrance to a compartment of the garden, while beautifully laid-out patterns of neat, small-leaved evergreens, such as box (*Buxus sempervirens*), were filled in with gravel to provide a year-round pattern. This fashion then found favor in the great estates in England until, in the eighteenth century, the landscape gardener Lancelot "Capability" Brown swept away such conceits in favor of a naturalistic approach.

Since then topiary has waxed and waned in popularity, but it has always had its devotees. At its most complex, topiary can prove an extremely time-consuming art. The plants used for classical topiary are small-leaved and slow-growing, so it can take many years to achieve a large finished shape. Despite this, whole gardens have been based on topiary forms and shapes while others devote sections to virtuoso topiary skills, such as the famous chess set at Haseley Court in England. In yet

other gardens, a whimsical approach to topiary has been used. At Marilyn Abbott's garden in Hampshire, a small knot garden has been laid out with an *Alice in Wonderland* theme, complete with topiary characters drawn from the book.

For those with small gardens, even as small as a balcony or windowsill, the neatly clipped outlines of topiary can offer an air of elegance and formality. From little box balls in small terra-cotta pots arranged neatly on a window ledge to a pair of pom-poms flanking a doorway, topiary in containers gives our houses and gardens the perfect finishing touch.

There are many specially made wire frames to be found for a wide variety of simple topiary shapes; these are used as an overall guide when trimming the shrub, making it easier to produce a neat outline and reducing the need for any great design skill. A number of suppliers (see page 94) will furnish you with all manner of topiary frames, from simple obelisks to fancy beasts, and from little teddy bears to elegant swans.

Topiary forms can be created just as easily in containers as they can in gardens. You will, of course, need to feed and water the plants frequently and clip and train them as assiduously as you would in the garden, but otherwise they do extremely well. One great advantage is that you can turn the pots so that any uneven growth caused by the shoots growing toward the light can be corrected.

Apart from the traditional shapes and the plants used to create them, there are new forms of topiary with which to experiment. For the less patient, quick-growing ivy (*Hedera* sp.) presents an opportunity to create topiary shapes in months rather than years. For those prepared to exercise their imagination, almost any shape or idea is possible, and there is a broad range of plants that one can use (see Directory of Plants, pages 86–92).

left: *In this London garden, the clipped formality of box, much of it in containers, helps to contain and give shape to the garden. Large pots with underplanted box standards mark the entrance to the lawn, and the path is flanked on one side with a line of gaily striped containers of box balls.*

CHOOSING THE FORM that you wish your topiary to take is half the fun, since the choices are so varied. It makes sense, however, to opt for some of the simpler shapes until you are more familiar with the art and perhaps to create a couple of fast-growing topiaries from ivy alongside one or two more slow-growing traditional forms, so that you enjoy a more rapid result from your efforts.

It pays to consider where you are going to display your topiary before you start, so that its shape and size is appropriate for the location. If you want to create a matching pair of topiary containers for a doorstep, for example, then it might be better to choose a slender, elegant shape, such as a pyramid or perhaps a large rectangle. You could create them from either box or privet (the latter is faster-growing than box but it will need more frequent clipping and shaping) or, for speed, from ivy.

In addition to the classic shapes, there are plenty of interesting shapes to choose from (see pages 24–47). You could even personalize your topiary by creating your own initials.

If you want to create a topiary display, combining different shapes and sizes adds to the overall impact. Some of the most successful window-box designs feature two small box balls flanking a slightly taller central pyramid. By putting a pair of matching topiary window-box displays on the sills of your windows, you help to emphasize the symmetrical nature of the architecture. Although it can look attractive to interplant the more sober topiary forms with flowering plants, you need to do this with care so that the simplicity of the topiary (its chief attribute) is not overwhelmed. Keep the subsidiary planting simple, ideally with a single color theme, and avoid too many trailing plants.

right: *Many gardeners are justifiably proud of their topiary creations. These beautifully clipped and maintained wedding cake tiers, peacocks, and pyramids, on elegantly shaped bases, are brilliant examples of topiary art at its best.*

TOPIARY
techniques

Most fairly simple topiary shapes do not demand great skill to create, but you should make sure that you maintain the plants in full vigor at all times for the topiaries to look their best. This chapter explains how to choose and decorate the containers, the kind of topiary frames you can buy or make to provide a guide for growing and training your plants, and how to perform basic cultivation, including feeding, watering, general maintenance, and propagation.

right: *This selection of terra-cotta containers includes both plain and textured pots. The size and style of the topiary will determine the form you choose. Small topiaries in miniature pots can be lined up on a path or windowsill to create an effective display.*

CONTAINER SHAPES AND SIZES

ONE THING IS CERTAIN: If you are going to make the effort to create your own topiary, you must take the time to choose appropriate containers. The elegant forms of the topiary shapes demand good-quality containers, and the overall size of the container must be appropriate for the size and scale of the topiary concerned.

There are various good-quality materials to choose from, and many ready-made containers can be found in interesting shapes and sizes. The classic materials and shapes are often the most successful, but some interesting new ideas have come into play recently, in particular the recycling of industrial materials, the minimal style of which seems to go very well with the stark, spare outlines of the topiary it contains.

When looking at proportion, bear in mind that the size of the container should, generally speaking, be one-third of the height of the finished topiary. This creates a reasonably attractive balance, but rules are made to be broken, and there may well be a case for surmounting a large container with quite a small topiary, although the opposite rarely applies—it usually looks slightly ludicrous, like a large person with very small feet.

terra-cotta

This is the most widely used, and probably most widely available, material for containers. It has become increasingly popular over the years, and you can buy fine hand-thrown pots or machine-made, mass-produced ones. Shapes and sizes vary from simple Long Tom pots (with no lip) to more elaborate ones with a raised design. Generally speaking, the plainer the pot, the more appropriate it is, in order to emphasize the architectural lines of the topiary itself. Hand-thrown pots have a wonderfully soft, delicate hue but the machine-made ones, while inexpensive, have a bold color when new, although they will weather in six months to a less intimidating color. You can speed up the process by artificially aging them (see page 16).

metal

The traditional metal containers were made of lead (difficult to lift, and now too valuable to place in the garden), but modern containers in anodized aluminum or matte steel can be very effective and would certainly look good on the windowsills, terrace, or balcony of a modern home. You can buy large planters— rectangular or square—or various rounded shapes, from cylinders to ellipses, which will give the topiary a modern touch. You can play around with the shapes of the pots and topiaries, putting a ball-shaped topiary in a square pot, or vice versa, to add to the visual interest.

wood

There is a wide range of wooden tubs and window boxes available. The classic rectangular tub with finials at its four corners is known as the Versailles tub because it is a copy of the pots to be found at the famous French château garden of that name renowned for its parterres. Good-quality wood containers will last a long time and their longevity will increase if you use a plastic liner inside the container. Don't forget to puncture its base to allow for drainage. Some trendy modern containers have been created out of humble orange boxes, so nothing is sacred when it comes to making containers!

below (left): *Metal containers are a good match for geometric topiaries in modern settings.*

below (right): *Wooden containers—a Versailles tub made from bamboo and a slatted wooden trough are shown here— are always a popular choice for balconies and doorways.*

DECORATING CONTAINERS

IF YOU WISH, you can customize your containers in various ways to make them look more interesting. Anthony Noel, one of London's leading small-space garden designers, painted some of his with stripes (see page 27). In fact, he painted so many that he said he eventually grew sick of them, but a simple painted motif that is repeated on a row of small pots containing young box plants, awaiting their eventual transmogrification into topiary specimens, makes a nice display out of your plant nursery. Simple designs suit the formal nature of topiary best. One easy method is to stencil a small motif onto each pot using gloss varnish.

Modern machine-made terra-cotta pots often have a lip at the top of the pot, which could be painted in a contrasting color, or you can create your own band of color on a flat-sided pot (see opposite).

If your pots, whether metal or terra-cotta, look too new, then consider artificially aging them to give them a more naturally antique appearance. Metal pots can be given a verdigris effect with separate coats of blue and green paint speckled onto the surface and then sealed with acrylic varnish. For terra-cotta pots, use the simple aging technique shown below.

How to age a terra-cotta pot

All you need to age a brand-new terra-cotta pot in a matter of weeks (rather than the months it normally takes) is a carton of yogurt and a small paintbrush.

1 Coat the container liberally with a thin layer of yogurt, revolving the pot on its base as you apply the yogurt.

2 Leave the container to dry for several hours, then pot up in the usual way. The above effect took three weeks to achieve.

How to decorate a terra-cotta pot

To create this simple but effective band of color around the top of a Long Tom terra-cotta container, all you need is a colored pencil, some masking tape, a small pot of exterior gloss paint (forest green in this case), and a paintbrush.

1 With the pencil held between your thumb and forefinger and resting the tip of your finger on the pot edge, draw a line around the pot.

2 Apply masking tape to the edge of the marked ring around the top of the pot. Press the tape down against the sides of the pot along the drawn line.

3 Using a fine brush, coat the edge of the pot neatly with paint, being careful not to allow the paint to go over the edge of the rim.

4 Allow the paint to dry thoroughly before carefully peeling off the masking tape.

TOPIARY FRAMES

below: *Made with galvanized wire, these are two of the simplest frames you could choose for your topiary, which can be made from either slow-growing box or other small-leaved evergreen shrubs (see pages 88–92), or from quick-growing ivies for a faster result.*

FRAMES ARE USED AS a guide for clipping and training topiary, and are generally simple wire constructions over which the plants can be trained. Some of the most popular shapes are rabbits, dogs, squirrels, chickens, peacocks, and swans, but all kinds of beasts, real or mythical, can be conjured up for the purpose. Frames for simple shapes, wider at the base than the top, are usually removed after clipping; those for the more elaborate shapes are left in situ.

Topiary shapes tend to go in and out of fashion. Teddy bears are increasingly popular, as are whimsical shapes, and you can also look around in junkyards for odd objects, such as old car springs, around which to create modern topiary. Generally speaking, the less complex the outline, the quicker and easier it will be to create a realistic and satisfactory final effect.

The topiary does not always have to fill or cover the frame entirely, and some very attractive effects are created by allowing a few shoots of a pretty flowering climber to scramble over an intricately designed wire sphere (see page 58). To achieve a balanced appearance, make sure that you choose an appropriate-sized container for the frame you have in mind.

making your own frames

If you wish, you can make your own simple wire frames, for which you will need heavy-gauge wire (galvanized, copper, or plastic-coated), a pair of wire cutters, and a pair of pliers, as well as some reel wire for joining lengths of wire. To create a simple globe, for example, you can use suitable objects, such as old flower pots, around which you can bend the wire into a simple circle. Two circles of the same size with a small "tail" wire at the joint complete the structure. Chicken wire can be used to cover the shape if you then want to make a fully covered globe (see page 62). Remember to use gloves when cutting chicken wire—it is very sharp.

left: *Some topiary frames are so beautifully constructed that they make sculptural elements in their own right. These two dogs are almost too good to serve as growing guides!*

below: *Animal and bird shapes are popular and also fun to grow. Smaller shapes will achieve their final forms quite rapidly if you use plants that are already well grown.*

BASIC CULTIVATION

YOUNG PLANTS FOR TOPIARY can be purchased from a garden center or nursery. Your choice of plant will be determined by the style of topiary you have in mind. Neatly clipped forms require plants with small evergreen leaves; standards require trees, shrubs, or perennials with a woody stem; and false topiary needs quick-growing climbing plants.

All plants need adequate light—although some, such as ivy, will do fine with less. Remember to position those plants that need a good amount of sunlight in the right place (see individual plant entries on pages 88–92 for information on appropriate conditions).

equipment

Apart from the basic pots and multipurpose potting compost, you need very little basic equipment for topiary apart from a pair of good-quality pruning shears and a pair of garden scissors. You will also need a watering can.

planting

When you plant, you must use clean pots large enough to give the rootball space to grow (a diameter 3 in. larger than that of the rootball is the norm). The pot must have adequate drainage and, if you use some kind of found object (such as a metal bucket) as a container, remember to drill holes in the base for this purpose. The holes should then be covered with some shards of broken pots, or with large pebbles, so that they do not become blocked with compost and so that the compost does not wash away when the plant is watered.

To plant up, fill the pot one-third full with a multipurpose potting compost, spread out the roots of the plant to be potted, and position it so that the crown of the plant (where the stem starts) is level with the top of the soil (about 1 in. below the surface of the pot to allow room for watering). Firm the compost down well with the heels of your hands. Water thoroughly and add a mulch to the surface (pebbles or mussel shells are ideal) to prevent future moisture loss.

opposite: *A selection of evergreen cuttings, including lavender, box, yew, and rosemary. If you use several cuttings, there is a better chance that at least one will grow to maturity. Most cuttings take about 10–12 weeks to root, during which time they must be kept moist but not waterlogged.*

above: *A mulch of gravel over the surface of the compost will help to reduce moisture loss and keep weeds from growing.*

above (left): *Fertilizers often need to be mixed with water before use. For the best results, carefully dilute the feed according to the manufacturer's instructions.*

above (center): *Water plants regularly to ensure that they do not become stressed, aiming to keep the compost moist at all times.*

above (right): *To ensure you clip topiary evenly on all sides, you can use a metal or wood frame for the shape required, clipping only those shoots that protrude beyond its outline.*

feeding

This is an essential element in creating container topiaries, since the aim is to get the plants growing as vigorously as possible. Bear in mind that the nutrient content of the compost you used for planting up lasts for only a few weeks. After that you will need to feed the plant roughly once a month while it is actively growing (spring to fall). In order for the plant to be able to take up the nutrients, the compost must be moist, so regular watering is also essential.

Various types of feed can be used, from a simple dressing of homemade compost (well-rotted vegetable matter) to store-bought fertilizers that are specially formulated for certain plants. Quick pick-me-ups can be provided with foliar feeds, which are sprayed directly onto the leaves, and you can also buy slow-release fertilizer granules that cut down on the frequency of feeding.

watering

Some plants are more drought-resistant than others. Lavender and rosemary, both useful plants for training into standards, can cope without water for longer than many other plants, and ivy (the most popular quick topiary plant) also copes well without much water, but less water will slow down their growth.

You can tell whether the plant needs watering by familiarizing yourself with the weight of the container. A recently watered container is surprisingly heavy; one that is suffering from drought is lighter. (You can buy moisture-gauge sticks that give a reading that indicates whether watering is necessary.) If you have let the container dry out, then plunge the pot and the plant within it into a bucket of water and leave it there until the bubbles stop rising. Most of us water too little, but overwatering can also be a problem. The compost should be moist, not constantly soaking wet.

general maintenance

The techniques for clipping and shaping the plants are covered in the individual entries. However, you will also need to take care of your plants in the winter if they are tender (see Directory of Plants, pages 86–92) and if you live in a cold climate. Those that are somewhat frost-tolerant can have their pots wrapped in burlap or bubble wrap in the coldest months. Tender plants will have to be brought indoors once the frosts start.

Keep any tools you use for clipping and pruning sharp and well oiled, as torn cuts are likely to encourage diseases, as well as making the plants themselves look untidy. There are, unhappily, quite a few pests and diseases that may attack your handiwork. You can guard against them, to some extent, by making sure that you keep the plants well watered and well fed, and that they are in conditions where the air can circulate reasonably well.

simple propagation

Although container-grown plants are expensive to buy, many of them can be raised relatively easily from cuttings—small shoots removed from the parent plant. Box generally grows very easily from cuttings, so you can raise a whole forest of topiary plants if you have the space. Information on the various types of cutting appropriate for different topiary plants, and when to take them, are given in the individual plant entries on pages 88–92.

How to take a box cutting

Box is one of the principal topiary plants and one of the easiest to propagate. It will grow well from a small shoot (about 4 in.) removed from a stouter stem with a small heel of bark. Prepare a small pot by filling it with a mixture of potting compost and a handful of grit.

1 Remove a suitably sized cutting from the parent plant, pulling away a small heel of bark from the stem as you do so.

2 Insert the cutting into the compost to a depth of about 1 in. Water the pot and keep it moist (cover it with clear plastic to conserve moisture).

SIMPLE
shapes

Some of the most effective, and the most popular, topiary shapes are those based on simple geometry—balls, cubes, and pyramids. This chapter shows you how to create these basic shapes from small-leaved evergreens, such as box, using well-grown young plants. If you create a matching pair, they are ideal for framing a doorway. You could also use a line of small topiary balls to define a path or a flight of steps.

SOMETIMES THE SIMPLEST and easiest shapes—geometric cubes, balls, and pyramids—are the most effective. However, they will need to be properly cared for and well trimmed to look good, as any browned or wayward shoots will be particularly obvious.

The classic topiary plants are the best choice for simple shapes: box, privet, and yew are ideal for balls, squares, or pyramids, as the small, dark evergreen leaves produce a neat, clear outline.

Some people prefer to use a frame as a cutting guide when trimming topiary, but you can often manage to trim small, simple topiary shapes by eye. However, you need to work carefully, in stages, as it is only too easy to keep snipping bits off until very little remains! When trimming these shapes, you need to turn the topiary as you work so that the result is even. If you are trimming several topiaries that will be displayed together, it is helpful to use a frame to ensure that they all achieve the same size and form.

The small, simple shapes have the greatest impact when displayed in groups, either using repeating motifs of the same shape or combining them in symmetrical formations, such as a pyramid flanked by two balls or perhaps four square topiaries to mark the intersection between two paths.

If you wish, you can use a central small topiary shape to provide the mainstay of a window box, or of pair of window boxes, with softer planting that is renewed seasonally on either side of this year-round foliage feature. Small shapes look equally good lined up in rows on a windowsill, as a feature pair on top of gateposts, or positioned on either side of a door.

When creating grouped displays, make sure that you use matching materials for the containers, either by opting for one specific type, such as metal or terra-cotta, or by painting more disparate pots in the same color or in a range of toning colors. This is particularly important if you are grouping together a range of shapes to add some sense of unity to the display. Make sure that the container size suits the shape and scale of the topiary.

SIMPLE TOPIARY CUBE

THIS IS ONE of the least-complex topiary shapes, but its very simplicity can be slightly deceptive, as it relies on precise trimming and very dense foliage, achieved by frequent trimming over several seasons, to look good. The best plants to choose are box, in one of its many forms, privet (*Ligustrum* sp.), and yew (*Taxus baccata*), as these will all create the necessary dense foliage. Although you can trim the shape by eye, you will find it easier if you use a cube-shaped guide to ensure that the sides of the cube are as straight as possible.

Pairs of cubes can be used to flank displays of more elaborate topiaries. Make sure the dimensions of the cubes suit the scale of the other plants in the display. With their crisp outline, modern, minimalist containers suit them best.

opposite: *This neat box cube has been given a contemporary appearance with a container made from a recycled packing case, but a rectangular terra-cotta or stainless steel container would look more formal.*

How to create a topiary cube

To make a cube roughly 12 in. square, you need to grow the topiary (or buy a suitable plant) that has already reached roughly this height. A simple metal cutting guide of the size required will help to ensure an even shape. Plant up in a container at least as wide as the proposed dimensions of the cube. The topiary will need to be clipped twice yearly, in late spring and late summer, until the shape is achieved.

1 Position the cutting guide over the plant. Pinch out the topmost growth at the required height and then trim all the shoots by a few inches.

2 As the plant begins to bush out, remove any straggling shoots that protrude beyond the cutting frame. Supply regular doses of seaweed-based fertilizer to encourage growth.

3 Trim twice yearly. By the second season, the shape should be more or less achieved. Clipping in subsequent seasons will help to create a denser shape.

SIMPLE TOPIARY PYRAMID

THIS PARTICULAR SHAPE makes an extremely effective topiary, and is among the most popular, being both elegant and eye-catching. You can make topiary pyramids based on either a traditional three-sided pyramid or a cone. There are a number of evergreens that lend themselves to this form, including bay *(Laurus nobilis)*, privet, yew, and cypress *(Chamaecyparis sp.),* as well as the ubiquitous box *(Buxus* sp.) in its many species and varieties.

The rounded pyramid is the easier of the two shapes to construct and follow and can be cut by eye once the basic pyramid shape is achieved. A three-sided cone is best cut with a frame to ensure that each "face" of the cone is evenly shaped and sized.

How to create a topiary pyramid

Once you have grown a plant to roughly the right height and shape (use a store-bought frame to create the approximate pyramid shape), you can then clip it more tightly to its final shape. It will need to be trimmed twice a season, in late spring and summer, to keep its outline.

1 When the plant has grown to roughly the right height and it has been clipped to an approximate pyramid shape, nip out the tip of the leading shoot.

2 Start to make the first cut, working up from the base of the pyramid to the top, taking a small section of the plant and cutting back the shoots by the most recent growth.

3 Work your way around the pyramid a section at a time, and then finally clip it lightly all over once you have succeeded in achieving a well-balanced outline.

opposite (top): *A young topiary pyramid. As you clip it each season, it will gradually take on a denser shape, similar to the one shown at left.*

left: *This well-clipped box pyramid has a good, neat shape, achieved by regular trimming. The metal container and the gravel mulch used to cover the compost add a modern twist to a classical design.*

SIMPLE TOPIARY BALLS

above: *A series of small topiary balls, each in a hand-painted, striped container, are ideal for edging a path or patio.*

THESE SIMPLE LITTLE BALLS are relatively easy to create. Being small, they do not take years to grow into the required form. To achieve more impact, grow several and line them up in a row on a windowsill or to flank a path, or put them in pairs on a flight of steps. You can either buy a circular frame to act as a clipping guide or you can try to clip them free-form. Achieving an identical result for several balls may be more difficult and is best done using a frame.

The best plant to use for the smallest spheres is the very small-leaved box (*Buxus microphylla*). Larger ones could be created from privet (both golden- and green-leaved forms). For rapid results, go for the false topiary globe in ivy shown on page 62.

To add interest to a series of box balls, consider painting or decorating the containers in a colorful but suitably elegant design, such as the stripes shown here or with a glazed motif stenciled onto the pot and simply varnished.

How to create a simple box ball

You will need a plant grown to a height a few inches taller than the eventual height of the sphere, as this will create the shape much more quickly and will be easier to trim.

1 Grow the box plant, clipping it into a rough ball shape until it is about 2 in. more than the required circumference.

2 Tie a piece of tape around the widest part of the plant to the desired measurement. Start to trim around this guide.

3 Trim the plant in sections, starting with the top center. Clip the top sections and then clip from the center to the base.

FANCY
shapes

The range of topiary shapes you can create is limited only by your determination. Those shown on the following pages are all popular ones to create, and within the grasp of any amateur topiary fancier. Creating matched pairs of more elaborate shapes is more difficult because it is hard to be absolutely precise with measurements. Shapes in this section include spirals, pom-poms, a heart, a hen, and a peacock.

IF YOU HAVE caught the topiary bug, you will want to experiment with ever-more-elaborate shapes to show off your newfound skills. Some of the most popular are tiered pom-poms with a length of clear stem between each pom-pom. They vary in form from two simple, equal-sized pom-poms, stacked one on top of the other, to more elaborate "wedding cake" tiers.

Another popular fancy shape is the spiral, usually with four or five "twists." The proportions of the twists are a matter of choice—some have a more serpentine shape with wider cuts, in others a more densely formed spiral shape is preferred. The former creates a more vigorous, dynamic feel to the topiary; the latter is more geometric in shape and looks more formal.

Apart from the selection shown on the following pages, you can make your own composite shapes. For example, you could make a square-based topiary with a pom-pom shape directly on top of it, rather than leaving the usual length of clear stem.

It is best to display these fancy shapes in symmetrical pairs, or in company with other simple topiary shapes, which provide an attractive contrast to your more elaborate handiwork.

The smallest-leaved evergreens will give the neatest shape, so for fancy shapes, carefully pick plants that will show off the form to the best effect. Box, yew, and privet are the most commonly used for spirals and flatter pom-poms, but holly is a good choice for round, ball-shaped pom-poms.

Animal and bird shapes have long been popular for topiary. The easier ones to create are those with a simple body structure (such as a hen, peacock, or swan) that is clipped from the main growth of the plant. Shoots are then trained to create the head and beak at one end and the tail feathers at the other. Of the fancy shapes, the heart (on page 46) is popular and relatively easy to create.

below: *This terrace has an attractive mixture of topiary shapes, including pom-poms and standards. Varying the shapes and plants helps to create a more lively looking display.*

TOPIARY SPIRALS

FOR A MORE ELABORATE variation on the basic topiary pyramid or cone, you can create the illusion of a spiral-grown plant by cutting and trimming a pregrown topiary pyramid (see page 30) to the appropriate shape. You will either have to grow the topiary yourself to approximately the right height and form and then clip it into shape or you can buy a ready-made topiary pyramid. A healthy plant with even growth on all sides is a prerequisite for this shape. You need to give the topiary a quarter turn every couple of months to ensure that the shoots grow evenly on all sides. Once the topiary is clipped into the right form, it will need trimming with shears twice each summer to keep its shape.

opposite: A handsome box spiral forms the centerpiece in this topiary display, flanked by pom-poms and a simple box ball. It often pays to create one of the topiaries from a variegated form to give a lighter effect.

How to create a box spiral

Apart from a topiary pyramid that has one strong central stem, you will need a length of wide tape, sufficient to wind around the proposed topiary pyramid as a cutting guide. You will also need a couple of clips to hold the tape in place at the top and base of the pyramid.

1 When the topiary has reached the appropriate size, nip out the leading (topmost) shoot to prevent further growth. Trim the new growth to make an even, conical shape (see page 30).

2 Attach the tape to the base of the pyramid and wind it around, at evenly spaced intervals, from the base to the tip. Start to clip away the foliage on either side of the tape.

3 Once you have clipped the appropriate rough spiral shape, you can remove the tape. Trim the shape to the desired depth (trim all the way to the central stem for a more defined spiral).

TOPIARY POM-POMS

opposite: *The charm of these topiary pom-poms lies in the way in which they have been grouped. Staggering the heights of topiaries is one way to ensure that they are well displayed.*

THE EASIEST WAY to create a topiary pom-pom is to cut the shape out from an already-established topiary cone, in much the same way that a topiary spiral is created. If you do this, you are better able to achieve a really neat shape. If you continue to clip the pom-poms closely, they will bush out and become more dense, their form gradually improving over a couple of seasons.

The style of pom-pom can vary. Some are made with evenly spaced tiers, diminishing in size toward the top. Others consist of a round ball shape at the base with a clear stem, crowned by a much smaller pom-pom. You could also combine one of the fancy shapes with a pom-pom base.

How to create a topiary pom-pom

First, create a roughly cut topiary pyramid (see page 30) out of the chosen plant material, ideally an evergreen with neat, small leaves and a strong central stem. Decide on the number and thickness of the pom-poms you wish to create. They look best with a graduated appearance, the largest at the base. You will need a couple of lengths of tape.

1 First, mark off the areas that need to be cut back, and wind tape around the plant to form a cutting guide. Nip out the leading shoot of the plant to stop further growth.

2 Using pruning shears, start to clip out the branches between the proposed pom-poms, cutting back to the central stem.

3 Start to shape the pom-poms (in the same way as for the box ball on page 33), starting at the base and working up to the topmost pom-pom.

ANIMAL SHAPES

opposite: This little topiary hen is still growing into its shape. In another season or so, the head and tail of the bird will have grown to fill out the frame, as will the body. Frequent clipping will give it a denser appearance.

WITHOUT DOUBT, these are the most fun to create and surprisingly effective results can be achieved in a relatively short period of time. The quickest shapes to produce are those that are relatively simple and follow the normal growth patterns of the chosen plant. Those in which individual branches have to be trained to produce more elongated elements will take much longer, although they are not necessarily more difficult.

Hens and peacocks are popular shapes simply because they work so well—a topiary hen is shown below and a topiary peacock on page 45. A purpose-made wire frame is essential, and most good topiary suppliers stock them (see page 94).

How to create a topiary hen

You will need to purchase an appropriate wire frame of the required size. You can start this topiary with any size plant, but if you buy one that is already well grown, you will achieve the shape in much less time. You will need to trim it twice each season until the required shape is achieved.

1 Plant the chosen plant, grown to at least as tall as the basic shape, in the container of your choice. Position the cutting guide over the plant.

2 Divide the foliage into three parts, one each for the tail, head, and back of the hen. Tie in loosely using garden ties.

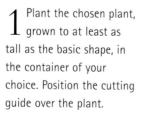

3 Clip the center part of the plant level with the hen's back and trim any straggling shoots at the tail and head that protrude beyond the frame. Then clip twice annually, using the frame as a guide until the frame is covered.

above and right:

A topiary peacock makes an attractive display. The little peacock (above) made from box is still growing into its frame; the peacock (right) from box-leaved honeysuckle (Lonicera nitida) has already done so, with its leading shoots forming the distinctive peacock's crown, and it is now ready for a final clip.

For a cockerel, you will need to allow one clump of shoots to grow out, so that it bushes out to make the tail feathers. This is also true of the peacock shown on this page, in which the shoots for the tail feathers are allowed to grow out and trained into a fan shape.

More elaborate animal shapes can be created simply by tying in sections of the plant while training others to extend in the direction required, often by using a training cane to which the extending shoots are attached. Animal shapes where the base consists of four legs, such as dogs, are best created using an appropriate number of plants. For a simple dog shape in which the two front and two back legs are blocked, two plants will do. For a more clearly four-legged shape you will need four plants. The plants are then trained in exactly the same way as the hen (see page 42).

How to make a topiary peacock

It is easiest to make this particular shape if you start with a well-grown, bushy plant with an adequate number of good branches to form the fanned-out tail. You can then use the peacock-shaped frame as a cutting guide. To encourage the plant to grow rapidly, use a good seaweed-based feed once a month in the growing season.

1 Plant up as for the hen (see page 42), and insert the frame. Then divide the plant into three equal parts—one for the head, one for the back, and one for the tail.

2 Clip the central part of the peacock back to the outline frame. Clip any protruding branches back from the tail and head ends of the peacock.

3 Keep clipping the body of the peacock back by roughly 4 in. each year, but clip the tail feathers by just an inch or so. By the third year, this should be fully grown and densely covered.

TOPIARY HEART

THERE ARE A NUMBER of ways that you can make a topiary heart. The one shown at right and below is a traditional box heart, shaped using a simple single-wire frame, but you can, if you wish, opt for one of the quick topiary techniques and make a similar shape very easily using ivy instead of box, tying in the new shoots as they grow as you would for the ivy globe or sphere (see pages 62–63).

If you prefer a more dense effect, you can purchase or make a heart-shaped frame with a 3-D appearance (it will have a couple of additional supporting wires running from the top of the heart to the base and around the center of the structure). You can then cover it with chicken wire, stuff it with moss, and grow ivy over the whole structure to form a completely dense shape.

If the shape stands well above the container, it pays to mulch the container to prevent weeds from growing, conserve moisture, and to give it a neater appearance.

opposite: This small topiary heart, measuring about 18 in. in height, has been made out of box trained around a galvanized wire frame.

How to make a topiary heart

You will need a simple heart-shaped wire frame. You can buy one ready-made or you can make it by inserting a nail on a board. Use this as the center point for the *V*-shape of the heart and then shape the heart by hand, twisting the wires into a tail to form a support. A well-grown box plant that will divide easily into two sections is needed as well.

1 Plant up the box plant in the usual way and insert the frame into the pot, making sure that it is firmly anchored in the compost. Divide the plant into two halves, tying each half into either side of the frame.

2 Keep tying the leading shoots into the wire frame. When they are long enough to reach the *V* of the heart, cross the shoots over and loosely tie them together.

3 Clip the shape twice a season. It will gradually thicken to cover the frame completely.

TOPIARY
standards

Standards—neat balls of flowers or foliage on top of a clear stem—make an interesting variation on topiary. Many different plants can be trained into this shape, from roses to holly. They can be used to add height to a group of plants in containers, or to add interest to a display of geometric topiaries. In matched pairs, they are the ideal plants for a doorstep, taking up very little of the available space. You can underplant them with seasonal flowers such as spring bulbs or summer bedding.

above: *Planting up a small standard in a large pot leaves room to grow flowering plants below. The display can be changed each season (pansies in winter, tulips in spring, busy lizzies in summer, and cyclamens in fall), while the foliage standard provides the central architectural feature.*

opposite: *Foliage standards are the ideal choice to create a feature display on a step, taking up very little of the available space. Their neat form provides year-round interest, with the architecture providing the ideal background.*

TRAINING PLANTS INTO STANDARDS, where a straight stem is surmounted with a bushy head of leaves, flowers, or fruit—somewhat like a lollipop—is becoming increasingly fashionable. The concept is not new; it reached its heyday in Victorian times. At first, this did not find favor with gardeners who felt the practice went against the natural order, but the popularity of standard roses helped make the technique more acceptable. Today most people are familiar with the concept of pruning roses into standards, but perhaps less so with the notion that almost any shrub with a strong stem can be trained into a similar lollipop shape.

The plants that lend themselves most readily to this treatment are certain highly floriferous shrubs, such as roses and fuchsias, so that the mop head atop the stem is a ball of blooms; and small-leaved evergreens, whose glossy foliage can be clipped to make a neat ball. Good candidates here are bay, myrtle, and viburnum (which has the bonus of scented flowers as well as attractive foliage), but there is a wide range to choose from (see pages 88–92).

While most standards are created from the simple expedient of removing the lower side shoots until a clear stem of the appropriate height is formed, and then removing the growing point so that the mop head is created at the top, grafting enables you to join species together to create something more unusual (see pages 56–57). This technique reached its height in the mid-nineteenth century with some very bizarre creations, including one display where weeping beeches were grafted onto mature cedars. Those of us limited to small-space gardening, and with containers as our only growing space, are unlikely to echo these particular follies, but the technique of grafting is not difficult and the joining together of two plants with different characteristics and attributes does widen the range of possibilities.

right: *A fuchsia standard makes an attractive summer display for a doorway. If you want a longer-lasting display, plant the container with smaller flowering plants during the different seasons.*

opposite: *Among the many plants that respond well to being trained into standards are woody herbs such as lavender and rosemary. Being evergreen, they provide interest all year—with the bonus of attractive flowers in the summer.*

FLOWERING STANDARDS

THERE IS A SURPRISINGLY wide range of flowering plants that you can train into a standard shape. By far the greatest number are shrubs, but you can also use some perennials, with the help of a stake to which the stem is tied, and some climbers, which will also need staking.

The most popular plants are roses and fuchsias, but there are some less usual shrubs and climbers that you can try. Viburnum, for example, makes a dense head of foliage with the bonus of white flowers (some species and hybrids are scented) from early to late spring. Herbs, too, can be trained into standards, rosemary and lavender in particular.

How to create a flowering standard

It is important to bear in mind that the plant will be encouraged to bush out only if the leading shoot (once it attains the required height) is pinched out (the topmost leaves removed). This encourages the remaining shoots to grow, creating the requisite mop head. While you need to remove branches to create the clear stem, you must leave small shoots in place to give the plant the opportunity to take up food.

1 Plant up an appropriately sized young plant with a strong central growing stem in the chosen container. Remove side branches, but leave some small shoots in place.

2 Pinch out the growing point of the central stem and the shoots and leave the topmost shoots unpruned. Tie in the main stem of weaker-stemmed plants to a central stake.

3 Continue to pinch out the leading shoot. Prune back the topmost shoots by about one third just after flowering. They will bush out to form a mop-head top.

FOLIAGE STANDARDS

FOR ARCHITECTURAL EFFECT, you can opt for standards created from evergreen shrubs. Trained into the typical ball shape, they look good all year round. Bay, a handsome evergreen with aromatic leaves, is one of the best known and makes a singularly elegant shape; it is often used as classic doorway sentinels. Bay was thought to guard the house against bad spirits.

Other good shrubs for training into evergreen standards are myrtle, with the bonus of scented white flowers, and holly (*Ilex* spp). There are many hollies to choose from, from the smallest spiny-leaved, dark green ones to more glamorous golden- or silver-variegated forms (see page 89). Their densely packed branches of foliage make neat mop heads of leaves, often with the bonus of shiny red berries. Citrus trees, with their neat, glossy, evergreen leaves, also make good subjects for clipping into standards but will need winter protection in colder areas.

PROTECTING STAKES

If you are using canes to support a standard while the stem is maturing, be sure to to cover the tips. Gardeners are particularly prone to eye accidents from uncovered stakes!

How to create a foliage standard

Choose a plant with a well-formed central stem at least 3 ft. tall. For a standard of this height you will need a container roughly 12 in. in diameter. Plants with weak stems will need staking, for which you will need a stout cane and some garden ties.

1 Plant up in the usual way and stake the central stem to a support, tying in at intervals with plastic garden ties. Once the stem is strong enough, the stake can be removed.

2 Remove any large side shoots from the main stem up to 12 in. below the top of the plant. When the plant reaches the chosen height, pinch out the leading shoot.

3 The following season, pinch out the leading shoot again, and keep trimming the side shoots just below it to encourage them to bush out and grow more vigorously. Clip the shape into the form of a ball.

left: *This variegated holly standard has made a handsome ball of foliage on top of a strong, clear stem. Hollies with gold- or silver-edged leaves are a good choice, as the paler-colored margins of the leaves help create a lighter effect.*

above: *This little weeping willow has been created from a low-growing willow* (Salix x caprea) *grafted onto a taller-growing willow main stem. It bears attractive catkins in the spring.*

GRAFTED STANDARDS

WHERE YOU WANT to obtain a particular mop-head effect, but the plant itself will not produce the requisite clear stem, you can graft two plants together. The plant that provides the base must have a naturally straight, strong stem, obtained from one central leader. Once it has reached the required size, it is trimmed back and the stem of the new plant is then grafted onto the uppermost part of the stem of the base plant. There are a number of different grafting methods that can be employed, but the one shown below is easy enough for an amateur to copy. Among the many plants that are grafted are roses, in which a more vigorous rootstock is used for the supporting stem and a very floriferous rose for the mop head. An unusual combination is a small willow standard, in which a more vigorous rootstock provides the support for a pretty weeping variety.

GRAFT UNION

This close-up shows the graft union between the two plants that have been joined together to make the standard willow.

How to create a grafted standard

By cutting into the bark, you expose the layer known as the *cambium*, whose healing properties allow the stock and the scion (the plant being grafted onto the stock) to knit together.

1 Make a single upward, slanting cut about 2 in. long at the base of the top section of the plant and a matching cut on the bottom section of the rootstock.

2 Position the two cut surfaces of each plant so that they match. Once they are in position, bind them with an elastic band.

3 Put the newly grafted plant into a pot of compost and keep the grafted area moist (cover it with a plastic bag) until the wound heals.

QUICK
topiary

In addition to classical topiary, you can create imaginative topiaries from quick-growing plants such as ivies and other fast-growing climbers, or from pots of flowering plants such as pansies, scillas, and small tulips, built up to echo geometric topiary forms. You can even trim grass to make topiary-style features such as benches or chairs.

opposite: *This tulip tower has been built up using a series of stacking pots (see page 70 for instructions). The effect is similar to topiary, but obviously short-lived. It can make a splendid feature for a few weeks, and is a great conversation point for a special occasion.*

FOR THOSE OF US who are too impatient to wait several seasons for slow-growing plants like box to grow into the required topiary shape, there are other options. Quick-growing climbers, such as ivies, can be trained to cover traditional topiary wire forms, such as pyramids, spheres, and spirals, or some of the more fantastic ones, such as beasts and birds. Another alternative is to use climbers to partially clothe an attractive wire frame, which creates an almost sculptural effect (see page 58).

Fast-growing climbers will mature surprisingly quickly, covering a small frame in one growing season, and a larger one in a couple of seasons. You will need to pay particular attention to the way you care for this more unusual type of topiary, since the key element is that it looks good and retains its shape, an essential ingredient in the overall design.

In addition to the classic forms of topiary, there are inventive and original designs you can employ using fast-growing climbers or structures that produce a topiary-like shape using flowers. These novelty shapes can vary from topiary chairs and benches, created from neatly clipped grasses and herbs, to slender columns of flowers, for example pansies or tulips, built up in a series of containers to form pyramids or cylinders. The aim of these designs is to produce a formal effect and a neat, even appearance, so they need to be constructed carefully. While foliage topiaries are evergreen, creating year-round features in the garden, a flowering topiary has a relatively short season of interest but is a showstopper while in bloom.

By choosing more unusual plants or styles for topiary, you can add life and interest to the garden, as well as an element of fun. Although the origins of topiary are classical, it has always offered its practitioners an opportunity to experiment and release their creativity, as the herds of topiary sheep or the hunt in full cry in some of the great country house gardens attest.

Trained trees and shrubs (kept at miniature sizes by ensuring the roots do not grow), known as bonsai, are another type of topiary. An art form in Japan, these small, formal, clipped plants make attractive features for tabletops and balconies and can be bought ready grown in many good garden centers, the only requirement being to maintain them with regular clipping.

FALSE TOPIARY GLOBE

YOU CAN EITHER create an open frame for this little topiary ornament, growing the ivy only over the uprights (opposite) or you can cover the entire structure (left) with chicken wire to create the sphere. Much depends on the setting you have in mind for it. Whichever you choose, they look good as a matching pair, perhaps framing a trough of flowering plants, or you could set them on a pedestal or atop a pair of gateposts.

The best ivies to use for smaller-size frames are those with small, neat leaves, such as 'Pedata' or 'Conglomerata,' as the scale is better suited to the frame. Equally good are the variegated ivies such as 'Goldheart,' which produce an attractive, ethereal effect.

above: *This ivy sphere was made using a chicken-wire and moss form.*

The size and shape of the globe will determine how many ivy plants you need to cover it. If you wish to cover the entire globe, you will get the best coverage using about six plants for a sphere roughly 24 in. in diameter. For the small open globe shown here, four plants were sufficient.

How to create an ivy globe

For the ivy globe, opposite, you will need some young ivy plants (around 6 in. tall—ivy grows very quickly from cuttings) and a globe frame made from two circles of wire. If you wish to create the dense ivy sphere (above), then add horizontal wires on which to train the shoots.

1 Select a suitably sized container that balances the size and shape of the globe. Fill the pot two-thirds full with potting soil. Plant the ivy plants around the perimeter of the pot.

2 Insert the globe frame and start to train the shoots up each upright, twisting them around the wire supports. Tie the shoots loosely with plant ties, if necessary.

3 As the stems grow, continue twisting them around the frame. Once they have fully covered the frame, you can snip off the growing points and trim the ivy at intervals with pruning shears to keep it in shape.

left: *The little globe in its first season. The shoots will gradually flesh out the shape more distinctly as the straggling shoots are tucked in or snipped off.*

right: *A small ivy pyramid makes the ideal choice of topiary for a shady corner, as few other plants will grow as well in this location. This little pyramid is in its first year of growth.*

opposite: *A small pyramid created from a mixture of ivy and clematis. Even in its early stages, the pyramid still has a nice shape.*

FALSE TOPIARY PYRAMID

JUST LIKE THE BOX pyramid shown on page 30, ivy pyramids lend a classical feel to any garden. Since they are relatively quick growing, they are a good means of achieving height in a planting scheme, particularly if the container in which they are set is above ground level. For larger pyramids, you can choose ivies with larger leaves, such as 'Glacier.' For quick results, use those that grow fast (see page 89). Almost all ivies, except those with variegated leaves, will cope well with very low light levels, so a pyramid composed of them is the ideal choice for a shady balcony, porch, or backyard.

The pyramid shape is an easy one to construct yourself (see below). For good coverage, it pays to make one out of chicken wire and fill the shape with moss.

How to make an ivy pyramid

For the topiary pyramid shown at left, you will need three good-sized, small-leaved ivy plants (about 8 in. tall) and a suitably sized container (around 12 in. in diameter and depth). You will also need a pyramid-shaped frame, some reel wire, and a pair of scissors.

1 Plant up the container with the ivy plants evenly spaced around the perimeter. Insert the pyramid-shaped guide over the container.

2 Using reel wire, crisscross the struts of the frame to provide additional support for the ivy shoots as they grow. Keep the plants well watered and fed to encourage growth.

3 As the plants grow, train them by twisting them around the struts of the frame. Once the frame is well covered, the ivy can be clipped to create a dense, neat shape.

FALSE TOPIARY SPIRAL

AS MOST CLIMBING plants are vigorous, they will quickly cover a tall frame, such as a spiral, in one or two seasons. Ivy is the most popular choice, as it not only grows fast but bushes out well, rapidly disguising the metal frame. There is no complicated pruning or shaping with false topiary forms—all you have to do is train the new shoots around the curves of the frame, tying in the more wayward ones using plastic plant ties and tucking any smaller strays into the general growth. Among the more rapidly growing ivies for this kind of topiary are cultivars of *Hedera helix*, such as 'Congesta,' 'Erecta,' and 'Pedata.'

If you wish to make your own spiral frame, you can do so by winding a few lengths of heavy-duty wire around an appropriately sized cone. Then remove the cylinder and bind the lengths of wire together at intervals. Attach a couple of stout wires to the base to form an anchoring point.

opposite: This 4-ft.-tall topiary spiral was created using three ivy plants, the leading shoots of which were then trained up the spiral frame. Once the shoots fill the frame, they can be trimmed with garden shears a couple of times a year to keep the outline neat and dense.

How to make an ivy spiral

You will need a spiral frame, a suitable pot (for example, a 4-ft. spiral requires a pot 8 in. in diameter), and two to three ivy plants. Insert the frame in the chosen pot, making sure it is well anchored in the compost. Plant up in the usual way (see page 21), inserting the plants at the base of the first coil.

1 Once the ivy has started to grow upward, train the new shoots by tucking them under the existing ones or tying them in.

2 When the ivy reaches the top of the spiral and the wire frame is fully covered, clip the structure neatly a couple of times during the growing season.

right: Viola 'Jackanapes' is a small-flowered, purplish-blue and yellow pansy that is ideal for this kind of topiary treatment. Larger-flowered pansies do not keep their shape as well, and the flowers are too loose.

FLOWER PYRAMID

opposite: This is a completed topiary pansy pyramid in which three tiered pots are placed on top of each other. In a very short space of time, the plants will grow together and disguise the underlying pyramid structure.

AS WELL AS the more traditional false topiary made from fast-growing creepers such as ivy, you can make topiary-like pyramids from small flowering plants with a fairly lax growth habit. They can be planted up to echo the formal topiary pyramid shape, using a tiered arrangement of three pots, with the largest at the base and the smallest at the top. They make an attractive and sympathetic addition to an evergreen topiary display, although they are not a permanent feature and will last only as long as the normal flowering season of the plant. Once the flowering season is over, dismantle the structure and feed and water the plants well until they are ready the following year.

Among the best plants for this kind of treatment are small-flowered pansies (*Viola* sp.), *Bacopa* sp. (which produces a looser effect), and little grape hyacinths (*Muscari* sp.). The secret to keeping the display looking good is to make sure that it does not suffer from excessive heat or drought. Keep it in partial shade and water it well at all times. Feed once every two weeks to prolong flowering, and remove dead flowers to encourage new growth.

How to create a flower pyramid

You will need to assemble three pots, ideally with a difference in diameter of about 2 in. each. The largest should be about 8 in. across and the smallest 4 in. in diameter. Approximately eighteen young pansy plants should be sufficient for this size of structure. You will also need enough potting medium to fill the three pots, as well as a small trowel.

opposite: *A less-formal version using the same principle but with* Bacopa *'Snowflake' as a substitute for the pansies.*

1 Start to build the underlying structure. Half-fill the largest container with compost and position the next container in the middle. Partially fill the sides with compost.

2 Start to add the individual plants around the base of the second pot (about five or six will be sufficient for this size of container).

3 You can then add the plants to the second container, around its edges, after partially filling it with compost.

4 Place the last pot in the center of the middle pot and plant it up with one or two plants as needed. Water it thoroughly and keep it well watered and fed.

TOPIARY CHAIR

opposite: *This ladder-back chair has had panels of foliage plants inserted into the seat and up the back. Occasional clipping will help create a neat, more sculpted appearance.*

ECCENTRIC FIGURES and fanciful items, from a chess set to a fox hunt complete with a fox, hounds, and horses, have long been the preserve of topiary specialists and can be seen in many of the great gardens. For those who want a slightly whimsical element to their topiary, but do not want to spend too long in the process, a simple topiary chair seat can be fun to create. The idea could be adapted easily for a bench as well.

The one shown here is created from chamomile (*Anthemis nobilis* 'Treneague'), which is a tough, small plant that makes a dense mat of foliage fairly quickly. It can be sat upon without doing it any permanent damage. As it is an herb, it is also pleasantly aromatic and has medicinal properties—if you are so inclined, you could make an herb drink out of the clippings!

How to make a topiary seat

You will need an old chair with a slot-in seat. For the seat you will need a board or piece of metal, punctured with holes and cut to fit the seat slot in the chair, some chicken wire cut to dimensions roughly 4 in. larger all around than the seat, a plastic liner, and a bucket of compost. To fill an 18-in. square, you will need approximately nine plants.

1 Put the board in the center of the chicken wire and turn up the edges of the wire to make a narrow surround. Cover this with black plastic with a few holes punctured in it.

2 Fill this with compost and plant up the plants at evenly spaced intervals. Water the plants well.

3 Transfer the board to the seat and fit it into the slot. Allow the plants to grow until they cover the compost, then trim twice a season in spring and summer.

DISPLAYING
topiary

Topiary can be used to enhance a variety of situations, from balconies and roof terraces to paths and flights of steps. Although the primary goal of topiary is to create an elegant classical display, its neat symmetry will help give unity and cohesion to more loosely organized groups of flowering containers, as well. You can use quick-growing evergreen climbers for false topiary to produce more rapid results.

THE WAYS IN WHICH you can use topiary vary greatly, but since its primary feature is its classic simplicity, it pays to introduce an element of formality into the design. Symmetrical designs are the most popular and are ideally suited to any formal setting. Pairs of container topiary pots are often used to flank a doorway or to mark the beginning of a path. Series of pots can be lined up on either side of a path, along a windowsill, or on top of a wall.

Since its form is its main attribute, you need to pay attention to the scale of the setting, ensuring that the topiary shapes enhance any architecture that frames them. Larger topiaries can be used to emphasize perspective or to draw attention to a vista or a view.

In less formal settings, topiary can be used as a focal point to bring a sense of cohesion and unity to an unruly mass of flowers, either with a single tall topiary feature or by containing more inhibited planting within a neat surround of geometric shapes.

More fanciful topiary shapes—exotic beasts and birds—can add humor and vitality to a more sober display, and they can act as a conversation piece on a patio or terrace.

The restrained and elegant lines of the topiary usually demand a similarly elegant container, but rules are made to be broken. If you want to play visual games, you can combine classic topiary shapes with surprising containers, galvanized steel window boxes, or recycled packing cases (see page 28) to produce a minimal, modern look.

right: *This front garden has made good use of different topiaries in containers to lend structure and dignity to the planting. A pair of box balls flank the front door, while tall clipped yews stand sentinel at the entrance to the path. Clipped hedging flanks the path, the curve of the stone ball contrasting with its neatly rectangular lines and echoing the shape of the box balls by the door.*

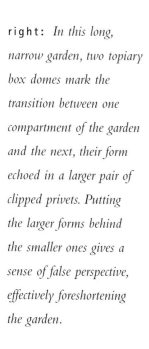

right: *In this long,
narrow garden, two topiary
box domes mark the
transition between one
compartment of the garden
and the next, their form
echoed in a larger pair of
clipped privets. Putting
the larger forms behind
the smaller ones gives a
sense of false perspective,
effectively foreshortening
the garden.*

FRAMING A VIEW

TOPIARY HAS LONG BEEN used in classical garden design to emphasize perspective and to make the most of long vistas. You can bring a touch of elegance to any garden by introducing neatly symmetrical pairs or groups of container topiary. Raising the topiary shapes on a plinth will help to add height, saving many years' growing time.

Useful design concepts include introducing contrasts of shape and form and positioning fancy spirals and pom-poms against the vertical lines of pergolas, columns, or doorways. Use smaller balls or pyramids in yew or box to lead the eye down a path toward a central focal point at its end.

below: In this classically inspired Irish garden, two matching pairs of handsome box spirals flank a small classical temple, drawing attention to its elegant lines.

DOORWAYS

THE ARCHITECTURAL FEATURES of your house provide an excellent setting for topiary—and few settings are better than doorways, which provide the ideal backdrop to a display of neatly clipped geometric shapes. The nature and style of the display will be dictated by the style of the architecture and the surrounding space.

If you have an elegant town house, for example, then a pair of matching pyramids in handsome containers are the perfect choice for the doorstep. A country house, with an expanse of terrace next to the door, allows you more scope and you can create a mixed display of pom-poms, spirals, cones, and pyramids (see page 39).

It is important to make sure the scale looks appropriate and, generally speaking, a handsome and imposing doorway is best set off with topiaries in a scale that does justice to it. Ideally, the height of the tallest topiary should be about one-third the height of the doorway (remember that the pot will take up roughly one-third of that height).

To create year-round appeal, you can put a pair of matching standards on either side of a doorway and underplant them with small flowering perennials or annuals, varying the display season by season, or use evergreen foliage plants for a more permanent display. Helxine, thyme, or chamomile can all be used to cover the surface of the container. If you decide not to plant up the container, then it is best to mulch the surface with some attractive material such as mussel shells or colored gravel.

BALCONIES

above: *A little topiary standard provides the centerpiece for a tabletop display, flanked by small architectural foliage plants in pots. Theming a display—in this case using foliage— helps to give it a sense of unity and cohesion.*

opposite: *Topiaries are ideal for balconies as they look good year-round and take up relatively little space. Combine them with luxuriant flowering climbers to achieve visual excitement with architectural elegance.*

THE SLENDER SHAPES of topiary standards and pyramids are ideal for small spaces. Not only do they lend an air of sophistication to the planting, they also help to emphasize the lines of the architecture. Since they are relatively easy to maintain, and both box and bay are fairly drought resistant, they are an attractive planting choice, yet exceptionally easy to look after.

If you create staging, such as a couple of wirework shelves, you will be able to give the planting additional interest by staggering the heights of the containers. Neat rows of box balls in matching pots on a simple shelf, with a flowering standard such as a fuchsia or rose positioned at each end, take up very little space while creating a display that is not only pretty, but durable. You can underplant the standards with short-lived displays of bulbs and annuals, ideally color-themed to give a sense of unity to the scheme—one such planting plan might be an all-white one of 'Triumphator' tulips in spring, followed by white busy lizzies in summer, white cyclamens in the fall, and white heathers in the winter months.

When underplanting topiary, you need to be careful to echo its simplicity of form so that the whole design looks harmonious. A stately topiary loses its effect if it is underplanted with blousy flowers. As the essence of topiary is understated elegance, this concept needs to apply to any subsidiary planting, too.

Ivies can be used to give a sense of movement to the planting if the topiary looks too static, but the smaller, dark-leaved ivies tend to combine better with it than the larger, floppier-leaved ones.

If you are planning to use quite large topiaries, or a fair number of them, it is important to consult a structural engineer to make sure that the balcony can handle the load successfully. Very high balconies may need some screening system to counter the effect of cold winds. You must also make sure that there is an adequate drainage system to carry away surplus water.

WINDOWSILLS

above: *A small window ledge houses a little terracotta window box with a tiny central topiary ball, in the process of growing to its full size, along with a variety of ivies and pansies.*

opposite: *For a modern setting, a straight-sided metal window box has been given an architectural treatment with ornamental cabbages planted on either side of a large box ball.*

IF YOU WANT an attractive, easy-to-maintain planting scheme for windowsills, you need look no further than topiary! You can choose from traditional topiary forms and plants or more modern ones, but the windowsill makes an ideal stage on which to display a collection of topiary. You can play with the combinations of shapes to achieve all kinds of interesting effects, whether all-foliage displays or combinations of foliage and flowers. The former can offer a sense of harmony and unity with different topiary shapes created from one type of plant (box is the most commonly used), or you can play with texture by using the same shape for each topiary, but using different plants. Some sense of symmetry is extremely important, however, as the geometric forms of topiary are lost without it.

One of the best schemes is to use a small topiary shape as the central plant in a window box and then change the flanking plants each season. This way the window box has structure but you enjoy the benefits of a changing display. For a very low-maintenance scheme, you can simply create rows of identical topiary shapes in attractive pots, be they plain terra cotta, metal, or subtly painted. Whimsical ideas include a series of playing card topiaries—a heart, diamond, spade, and club shape created from wire around which ivy is then trained.

Another successful solution is to alternate small pots of clipped box with similar pots of a single flower, such as the handsome dark-leaved, pink-flowered *Primula* 'Guinevere' or an elegant pansy like the nearly black *Viola* 'Mollie Sanderson.'

If you are growing your own plants from cuttings, you can plant each in its own small terra-cotta pot, lining up rows of these cuttings on the windowsill, perhaps painting the pots in alternating colors—white and black would produce a classical look. In this way, you succeed in using the available space to great effect.

If you are using several containers on a windowsill, make sure that they are of the same material or color, or are combined in some other appropriate manner. In a limited space every inch counts.

On higher windowsills, to prevent pots from being blown off the ledge (and possibly causing damage to other people or their property), it is a good idea to install some kind of restraining lip or, if you can afford it, an attractive railing.

DIRECTORY
of plants

Those plants commonly used in topiary, both for clipped forms and for training as climbers, are included on the following pages. The individual entries for each plant are in Latin name order. Each one includes the following information: common name (where applicable), hardiness, height in containers, suitable cultivars or varieties, position, cultivation, propagation, and any pests and diseases to which they may be subject.

ARGYRANTHEMUM FRUSTESCENS
Marguerite
Half-hardy
Height 4 ft.

Bushy, woody-stemmed perennials, marguerites have single, typical white daisy flowers with a golden central disc. The foliage is silvery green and finely divided. Cultivars come in different colors, including the bright pink 'Vancouver' and the yellow 'Jamaica Primrose' and 'Cornish Gold.' These plants make good standards. You will need to pinch out the shoot tips to encourage the head to bush out once the plant reaches the appropriate height. Marguerites prefer sun. You can propagate them from semiripe cuttings taken in early fall. Feed monthly with a seaweed-based fertilizer during the growing season. They are generally pest and disease free.

BUXUS
Box
Hardy
Height 4 ft.

There are several species of box, the best known being *B. sempervirens* (common box). It has small, oval, evergreen leaves. There are cultivars with variegated leaves, and the leaves also vary in size according to the species and cultivar. The smallest-leaved box is *B. microphylla*. Most grow to around 4 ft. but there are also dwarf and low-growing forms. Of the many cultivars of *B. sempervirens*, 'Handsworthiensis' is one of the best known. Being vigorous, it is a good choice for topiary as it will create the shapes you require more quickly than some other forms. It will put on 4–6 in. of growth a year. 'Suffruticosa,' which has small, neat leaves, is also used for topiary.

Box prefers sun or light shade and will cope with fairly minimal watering. You can propagate box easily from heeled cuttings taken in summer or early fall. Clip twice a year in early and midsummer for a neat finish.

Although box is easy to grow, it has recently become prone to attacks from a fungal disorder, for which there is no cure. It is less likely to succumb if grown with plenty of air circulating around the plant, and container-grown specimens seem to be damaged less than box hedges, particularly those that are grown under trees.

CEANOTHUS
California lilac
Half-hardy to hardy
Height 10 ft.

There is a wide range of species and cultivars, some evergreen, some deciduous, and some hardier than others. Choose the hardy evergreens for standards. *Ceanothus* 'Autumnal Blue' is a good choice with its small, dark evergreen leaves and its small, blue panicles of flowers from early to late summer. Of the deciduous ceanothus, you could try 'Gloire de Versailles' with its attractive dark blue flowers. Use either to make standards up to a height of 5 ft. The evergreen ceanothus will need only light pruning once the standard shape has been achieved. Deciduous plants should have the lateral shoots pruned back to a couple of outward-facing buds after flowering. Propagate from semiripe cuttings in summer. Ceanothus is fairly pest and disease resistant.

COPROSMA X KIRKII
'VARIEGATA'
Tender
Height 4 ft.

This tender, spreading, low-growing shrub would seem an unlikely candidate for training into a standard, but successful small standards can be created from it, with a prettily arching head similar to the willow (*Salix* x *caprea*) shown on page 56. The leaves are small and almost needlelike, a pale green edged with silver. If you grow a pair of male and female plants, mistletoe-like berries are

borne in the fall. It will need to be overwintered indoors in colder climates. The leading shoot of the standard will need to be staked to encourage it to grow straight. Feed the plant with a seaweed-based fertilizer at monthly intervals. Pinch out the shoot tips to encourage a more bushy head to the standard. Propagate from semiripe cuttings in late summer. They are generally pest and disease free.

x CUPRESSOCYPARIS LEYLANDII
Leyland cypress
Hardy
Height 10 ft. in containers

This is a very tough conifer that is quick growing, but it makes a good candidate for upright topiaries such as pyramids and spirals. The leaves are needlelike and glossy green. The compact, slower-growing *C. l.* 'Fletcheri' has grayish-green, feathery foliage. It should be planted in ericaceous compost as conifers prefer acid soil. It will need trimming two or three times annually, in spring and in early and late summer. It can be propagated from semiripe cuttings taken either in spring or in summer and it is generally pest and disease free.

CUPRESSUS
Cypress
Hardy
Height 10–13 ft.

These slender, upright, fast-growing conifers with their dense foliage make excellent topiary specimens and can also be trained as standards. There are forms with golden foliage, including *C. macrocarpa* 'Goldcrest.' Trains easily into pyramids, and can also be trained, less easily, into spirals. Plant them up using an ericaceous compost, as conifers prefer acid soil. Propagate in either early fall or spring from softwood cuttings. Cypresses are generally found to be pest and disease free.

Buxus sempervirens

Hedera helix 'Glacier'

Ilex aquifolium

FUCHSIA
Half-hardy to hardy
Height 5 ft.
These bushy deciduous shrubs, with small, oval, green leaves, are extremely floriferous with double or single flowers consisting of outer sepals with tubular dangling petals inside, often of a different color. Colors include carmine and purple, pink and white, deep cerise and pale pink. Different hybrids and species have varying degrees of hardiness. They make excellent standards but the stem will need to be staked. Of the many hybrids you can choose, 'Grandma Sinton' has pale pink semidouble petals and lighter pink sepals. 'Winston Churchill' has deep purple petals with rich pink sepals. They do well in sun or partial shade. Propagate from semiripe cuttings in summer. Prone to aphid attacks; spray with derris at the first signs of attack.

HEDERA HELIX
Common ivy
Hardy
Height 10 ft. or more
There are many different species and cultivars of ivy, a vigorous evergreen climber, but those that are most suitable for container growing for quick topiary are the more vigorous ones such as 'Erecta', 'Oro di Bogliasco', *H. h. pedata* and *H. h. f. poetarum*. Less vigorous varieties are 'Conglomerata' and 'Goldchild'. Those with small, neat leaves make good choices for more complex shapes, but the gold- and silver-variegated varieties, such as 'Goldheart' and 'Glacier', make an attractive alternative although their variegation may revert to plain-colored leaves in shade. Otherwise ivies do well in shady conditions. Ivy roots very easily whenever it touches soil, so propagation is simple—you can often detach an already-rooted stem or take cuttings in late summer. Ivy can sometimes be prone to red spider mites, but frequent misting with water helps prevent attacks.

ILEX
Holly
Half-hardy to hardy
Height 10 ft.
There is a vast range of species and cultivars in this group of trees and shrubs, which make excellent standards as the foliage is evergreen and very dense. Although we are familiar with the dark, glossy green spiny leaves of holly, there are many variegated forms, and some that have no spines to the leaves. Depending on their place of origin, hollies vary in hardiness. One of the most commonly grown is *I. aquifolium* (the common holly or English holly), which has many variegated cultivars. 'Argentea Marginata' has silver-variegated, spiny leaves. 'Golden Queen' has broad leaves with a dark green center and yellow margins. If you grow a pair of male and female plants, you will get bright red berries in autumn. Hollies do best in sun. Propagate from semiripe cuttings taken in summer. Hollies are fairly pest resistant but can be prone to powdery mildews.

LAURUS NOBILIS
Bay
Half-hardy
Height 10 ft.
This evergreen tree is deservedly popular for topiary and for standards. The oval, glossy, very dark green leaves are aromatic (and often used in cooking to flavor soups and stews). As a tree, it makes a strong, firm stem for a standard (which can be trained up to

Laurus nobilis

Lavandula officinalis

Ligustrum ovalifolium

6 ft. tall), generally putting on about 9 in. of growth a year, so it is fairly quick growing. It has small, inconspicuous yellow flowers in late spring, followed by small black fruits. In cold areas, you may need to provide winter protection by bubble-wrapping the container. It prefers a sunny position. Propagate from semiripe cuttings in summer. Bay can be prone to attacks from scale insects. Spray with malathion at the first sight of an attack (evidenced by the leaves starting to curl, with a white powdery substance inside the curled leaf), because it can quickly spread to the whole bush.

LAVANDULA ANGUSTIFOLIA
Lavender
Half-hardy
Height 3 ft.
This well-known herb with its evergreen, silver-green, needlelike leaves makes an attractive small flowering standard, although the head tends to be less spherical and the leading shoot will need staking to produce a strong stem. Depending on the hybrid or variety, small light- to dark-purple fragrant spires of flowers are produced from early to late summer. Lavender is a great attraction for bees. It prefers a sunny position. Propagate from semiripe cuttings in summer. Lavender is generally pest and disease free.

LIGUSTRUM OVALIFOLIUM
Privet
Hardy
Height 6 ft.
This tough evergreen is used widely for topiary. It is often used in place of box, being much quicker growing, but will need more regular clipping. There are gold- and white-variegated cultivars, such as 'Aureum' and 'Argenteum'. Plant in sun or partial shade. White, pungent-smelling flowers appear in summer. You can propagate it from semiripe cuttings in summer or hardwood cuttings in winter. Generally trouble free.

LONICERA NITIDA
Boxleaf honeysuckle
Half-hardy
Height 6 ft.
Similar in appearance to box, with small, dark evergreen leaves, but quicker growing. The golden-leaved cultivar 'Baggesen's Gold' is less vigorous and the leaves may scorch in strong sunlight. It will make good topiary specimens—ideal for pyramids—and is often used for standards. Small white flowers are borne in the summer, and purple berries in the fall. It will grow 6–9 in. a year, so will need clipping two to three times from summer to fall to keep topiaries in shape. It prefers sun (except for golden forms) or partial shade. Propagate from semiripe cuttings in late summer. Usually trouble free.

MYRTUS COMMUNIS
Myrtle
Tender
Height 6 ft.
This aromatic evergreen shrub is used for both topiaries and standards, the neat, small leaves being a dark glossy green and dense. It has the bonus of scented white flowers from early to late summer. Being tender, it will need protection in winter in colder climates. It prefers a sunny position. Feed with a seaweed-based fertilizer during the growing season. Clip after flowering. You can propagate it from semiripe cuttings taken in the summer.

Prunus sp.

Rosmarinus officinalis

Taxus baccata 'Elegantissima'

PELARGONIUM
Geranium
Tender
Height 6 ft. or more
There are various groups of pelargonium, but generally the zonal ones will make good standards. Tender perennials, but treated like annuals in cold climates, they have attractive, lobed leaves with markings in various colors from wine purple to white. The leaves release a pungent scent when crushed. The flowers are produced over a long period from early summer right through to the first frosts, and come in many different shades, from almost black through various reds and pinks to white. To train them as standards, you will need a conservatory or greenhouse as they will have to be overwintered. Propagate from shoot tips in summer and then grow the cuttings under cover in winter, removing the side shoots, but not all the side leaves, until the plant reaches the required height, when the leading shoot should be pinched out and the side shoots below it continually pinched until the mop head forms. Pelargoniums are generally trouble free, but the leaves will yellow if they are overwatered.

PRUNUS LAUROCERASUS
Laurel
Hardy
Height 10 ft.
A dense evergreen shrub, laurel has long, narrow, dark-green leaves with fragrant white flowers in the spring, followed by small red fruit (hence its other common name, cherry laurel). There are a number of varieties, including a variegated one, 'Marbled White' (formerly called 'Castlewellan'). It can be used to create mop-head standards or small topiary pyramids. It will do well in both full sun and partial shade. Prune it in spring. Prone to aphid attacks.

ROSA
Rose
Hardy
Height 5 ft.
This is a huge genus with a marvelous array of species and hybrid shrubs and climbers with flowers that range from single to double; some are very densely packed, known as "quartered." Almost all are richly fragrant. 'Ballerina', a hybrid musk rose, makes a neat standard with double pink flowers. While normal standards are up to 5 ft. tall, you can also grow patio roses as much smaller standards, only 2 ft. tall. You can also create weeping standards from climbers and ramblers, often trained over an umbrella-shaped wire frame. The technique for creating the standards is as for the fuchsia on page 53. Pruning will vary depending on the type of rose used for the mop head, but as a general rule cut out any diseased or crossing stems in late winter and then cut back any vigorous shoots to 6 in. and lateral shoots to about 4-6 in. in spring. Prone to black spot and to aphids.

ROSMARINUS OFFICINALIS
Rosemary
Half-hardy
Height 5 ft.
This aromatic evergreen shrub is also a much-loved herb. The small, needlelike leaves are glaucous gray-green, emitting a pungent aroma when crushed, and the flowers, from spring to early summer, are small, tubular, and pale blue-mauve. Rosemary can be used to create small flowering standards. You can propagate it easily from heel cuttings in

Thuja plicata 'Variegata'

Viburnum plicatum

Viola x *wittrockiana*

summer. It prefers a sunny spot, and will cope well with drought. Generally found to be trouble free.

SALIX
Willow
Hardy
Height variable
There are many different species and varieties of willow, which are characterized in the spring by attractive catkins and slender, often arching or drooping branches. For the purposes of topiary, train the creeping willows, such as *S. repens* (see page 57), to make small, attractively branched standards. Willows prefer to be kept moist in a sunny position. Can be attacked by aphids, caterpillars, leaf beetles, and sawflies.

TAXUS BACCATA
Yew
Hardy
Height 10 ft.
The common yew is a popular evergreen for topiary. It is slow growing and its very dark, needlelike leaves create a dense, uniform structure. The flowers are inconspicuous, but

small red (and poisonous) berries appear in fall and winter. Yew puts on about 8 in. of growth a year. It is well suited to topiary pyramids, which is in keeping with its natural growth habit. It will grow in both sunny and shady situations. Trim it back by 4 in. or so in summer and early fall. Generally found to be trouble free.

THUJA
Hardy
Height 13 ft. or more
This tough conifer is an evergreen, with very dark, scalelike leaves. It makes a good subject for topiary. Cultivars of species such as *T. orientalis* have the dense foliage necessary for an attractive topiary display. Some cultivars have golden foliage, such as 'Elegantissima.' *Thuja occidentalis* has foliage that is apple-scented. *Thuja occidentalis* 'Holmstrup' has green leaves. Plant in ericaceous compost in sun or partial shade. Trim back by 4 in. or more in spring and late summer. Can be prone to scale insects and also to attacks by aphids.

VIBURNUM
Hardy
Height 6 ft.
The evergreen species and cultivars make good standards. They have small, oval, dark-green leaves and flattish heads of tiny white or pinkish flowers in late winter or early spring. Some species have scented flowers. The flowers are often followed by small black fruits. *Viburnum plicatum* and *V. tinus lauristinus* make good standards. Plant in sun or partial shade. Propagate by semiripe cuttings in summer. Watch out for aphids and whiteflies.

VIOLA X WITTROCKIANA
Pansy
Hardy
Height 6 in.
Pansies make good subjects for instant floral topiaries, as the flowers will last over a long season; there are winter-, spring-, and summer-flowering pansies. They cope with partial shade but prefer sun. They need frequent watering and feeding. Grow from seeds sown in early spring. Can be prone to attacks by aphids and to mildews.

GLOSSARY

Annual *Plant that completes its life cycle in one season.*

Biennial *Plant that completes its life cycle in two years, growing in the first year and flowering and fruiting in the second.*

Cambium *Layer of cells between the bark and the wood that actively produces cells, and from which new cells will grow in the process known as grafting.*

Central leader *The vertical and dominant stem at the center of a tree.*

Crown *The upper branches and foliage of a tree.*

Cultivar *A cultivated variety of plant produced by horticultural plant breeding techniques.*

Deadheading *The removal of spent flowers to encourage more new buds to form.*

Deciduous *Plant that sheds its leaves annually at the onset of lower light levels and cooler temperatures.*

Dormant *The stage in the annual cycle of growth, usually in fall and winter, when the plant activity slows down or stops.*

Espalier *A form of training in which the lateral branches of a tree are trained horizontally.*

Evergreen *Said of a plant that is not deciduous, i.e., does not lose its leaves in winter.*

Family *A botanical term for a group of plants sharing similar characteristics.*

Fan *A form of training in which the lateral branches of a tree are trained at a 45-degree angle to the main stem.*

Genus *A subdivision of a family of plants, made up of species, hybrids, and cultivars that share closely related characteristics.*

Grafting *Process by which a shoot or single bud on one plant (technically termed the scion) can be united with the root system and stem of another plant (known as the rootstock or stock) to produce a plant that combines the characteristics of both plants.*

Half-hardy *Term used to describe a plant that is not reliably hardy, but may withstand temperatures just below freezing for short periods.*

Hardy *Term used to describe a plant that can withstand temperatures below freezing for longer periods of time.*

Hybrid *A cross between two or more species, denoted with an "x" in botanical names.*

Lateral *A subsidiary shoot growing from a larger stem.*

Leader
See Central leader

Pinching out *To remove the tip of a shoot; it prevents further growth of that stem and encourages laterals lower down to grow, creating a more bushy plant.*

Rootstock *The term used to describe the lower plant in grafting, which forms the roots of the combined plants.*

Scion *The term used to describe the upper plant in grafting, which is combined with the rootstock of another plant.*

Side shoot *A small shoot growing from a lateral or a main stem.*

Species *A subdivision of a genus, which can be further subdivided into subspecies, cultivars, and varieties.*

Standard *A tree or shrub trained to produce several feet of clear stem above which the upper branches are pruned into a ball shape.*

Tender *Term used to describe a plant that cannot withstand temperatures below freezing.*

Tipping *See Pinching out*

Variety *A naturally occurring variant of a species.*

TOPIARY SUPPLIERS

Bosmere Inc.
323 Corban Avenue SW
Concord, NC 28026
Tel: (704) 784-1608
www.bosmere.com

etopiary.com
1120 B Industrial Avenue
Escondido, CA 92029
Tel: (760) 738-9336
www.etopiary.com

Noah's Ark Topiary
P.O. Box 10213
Largo, FL 33773
Tel: (727) 393-8830
www.noahsarktopiary.com

O'Farrior Topiary
16415 Pleasant Beach Drive
Yelm, WA 98597
Tel: (360) 894-0825
www.otopiary.com

Pearsall's Garden Center
3100 Market Street
Wilmington, NC 28403
Tel: (888) GARDEN-1
www.pearsalls.com

Samia Rose Topiary
1236 Urania Avenue
Encinitas, CA 92024
Tel: (800) 488-6742
www.srtopiary.com

Simple Gardens
615 Old Cemetery Road
Richmond, VT 05477
Tel: (800) 351-2438
www.simplegardens.com

Thomson Topiaries
580 Crooked Lane
Barrington, IL 60010
Tel: (847) 304-0830
www.thomsontopiaries.com

Topiary Art Works
P.O. Box 574
Clearwater, KS 67026
Tel: (620) 584-2366
www.topiaryartworks.com

Topiary Inc.
42 West Watrous Avenue
Tampa, FL 33629
Tel: (813) 286-8626
www.topiaryinc.com

The Topiary Store
16307 115th Avenue SW
Vashon Island, WA 98070
(206) 567-5047
www.topiarystore.com

Zofia Design
1012 Skylark Drive
La Jolla, CA 92037-7733
Tel: (858) 459-0778
www.zofiadesign.com

FURTHER READING

Barbara Abbs
Climbing Plants
(Laurel Glen, San Diego, 2003)

Susan Berry
Kitchen Harvest
(Laurel Glen, San Diego, 2002)

Barbara Gallup and Deborah Reich
The Complete Book of Topiary
(Workman, New York, 1987)

Jenny Hendy
Quick and Easy Topiary and Green Sculpture
(Little, Brown and Company, London, 1996)

David Joyce
Topiary and the Art of Training Plants
(Frances Lincoln, London, 1999)

Nathaniel Lloyd
Garden Craftmanship in Yew and Box
(Ernest Benn Ltd, London, 1925)

John Raine
Garden Lighting
(Laurel Glen, San Diego, 2002)

Debbie Roberts and Ian Smith
Creating Garden Ponds and Water Features
(Laurel Glen, San Diego, 2003)

INDEX

a

animal and bird shapes 36, 42-45, *42*, 44, 60, 76

b

Bacopa 69, *70*

balconies 82, *82*

balls 26, *26*, 32–33, *32*, *39*, 60, 76, 79, *81*, 82, *84*

  false topiary globe 62, *63*

bay *6*, 30, 50, 54, 82, 89–90, *90*

bonsai 60

box 6, 9, 10, 26, 36, 82, 84, 85, 88, *89*

  animal and bird shapes 44

  balls 6, 9, 26, 32, 39, 76, 79, 82, 84

  cubes 29, 29

  cuttings 21, 23

  domes 78

  heart 46, 46

  pom-poms 39

  pyramids 30, 31, 79

  spirals 39, 39, 79

  standards 9

c

California lilac 88

chair 73, *73*

chamomile 73, 81

citrus trees 54

clematis *64*

clipping and shaping *22*, 23, 26

  cutting guides *22*, 26, 29

  see also individual shapes

companion planting and underplanting 10, *50*, 81, 82, 85

containers 14–17, 26

  decoration 16–17, 32, *32*

  drainage 21

  feeding 22

  metal 15, *15*, 16, 31

  planting 21

  proportions 14, 26

  recycled materials 14, 15, *29*, 76

  terra-cotta 14–15, *14*, 16

  wooden 15, *15*

Coprosma 88

cubes 26, *26*, 29, *29*

cuttings *21*, 23

cypress 30, 88

d

displaying topiary 10, 21, 74–85

domes *78*

doorways and entrances *52*, 81

e

equipment and tools 21, 23

f

false topiary 21

  flower pyramid 69, *69*

  globe 62, *63*

  pyramid *64*, 65

  spiral 66, *66*

feeding 22

fertilizers 22, *22*

flowering topiaries *52*, 53, 60, 68–71, *69*

foliar feeds 22

frames 9, *16*, *17*, 18–19, 42, 45, 46, 60

framing views 79

fuchsia 50, *52*, 53, 82, 89

g

grafting 50, *56*, 57

grape hyacinth 69

grouping topiaries 26, 36, *41*

h

heart 36, 46, *46*

helxine *6*, 81

history of topiary 6

holly 36, 54, 55, 89, *89*

honeysuckle *44*, 90

i

ivies 9, 10, 21, 22, 46, 60, 62, *64*, 65, *66*, 66, 82, 89, *89*

l

laurel 91

lavender *6*, *21*, 22, *52*, 53, 90, *90*

Leyland cypress 88

m

marguerite 88

metal containers 15, *15*, 16, *31*

moisture-gauge sticks 22

mulch 21, *21*, *31*, 81

myrtle 50, 54, 90–91

n

novelty shapes 60, 73, *73*

p

pansies 60, 69, *69*, 85, 92, *92*

ACKNOWLEDGMENTS

Susan Berry would like to thank the following for their contributions to this book: **Steven Wooster** for his excellent photography, **Debbie Mole** for her elegant design, **Kate Simunek** for her sensitive artwork, and **LeeAnn Roots** for help with styling. The **Langley Boxwood Nursery**, in particular **Geraldine Veitch** and **Elizabeth Bainbridge**, for supplying plants and for checking information and the **Wadham Trading Company** for supplying frames. Thanks also to **Rosemary Wilkinson** and **Clare Johnson** of **New Holland**, and to **Marie Lorimer** for compiling the index.